SandCastle™

First Rhymes

The Crook Can Cook!

Kelly Doudna

Consulting Editor, Diane Craig, M.A./Reading Specialist

ABDO
Publishing Company

Published by ABDO Publishing Company, 4940 Viking Drive, Edina, Minnesota 55435.

Printed in the United States.

Credits
Edited by: Pam Price
Curriculum Coordinator: Nancy Tuminelly
Cover and Interior Design and Production: Mighty Media
Photo Credits: AbleStock, Comstock, Hemera

Library of Congress Cataloging-in-Publication Data

Doudna, Kelly, 1963-
    The crook can cook! / Kelly Doudna.
        p. cm. -- (First rhymes)
    ISBN 1-59679-467-4 (hardcover)
    ISBN 1-59679-468-2 (paperback)
        1. English language--Rhyme--Juvenile literature. I. Title. II. Series.

PE1517.D6265 2005
808.1--dc22
                                                            2005049158

SandCastle™ books are created by a professional team of educators, reading specialists, and content developers around five essential components that include phonemic awareness, phonics, vocabulary, text comprehension, and fluency. All books are written, reviewed, and leveled for guided reading and early intervention reading, and designed for use in shared, guided, and independent reading and writing activities to support a balanced approach to literacy instruction.

Let Us Know

After reading the book, SandCastle would like you to tell us your stories about reading. What is your favorite page? Was there something hard that you needed help with? Share the ups and downs of learning to read. We want to hear from you! To get posted on the ABDO Publishing Company Web site, send us e-mail at:

sandcastle@abdopub.com

SandCastle Level: Beginning

-ook

book

brook

cook

crook

hook

This is a .

Here is a .

She can .

See the .

Look at the  .

The book is purple.

The brook is pretty.

Nan helps her mom
cook dinner.

The crook is mad.

The hook is yellow.

The Crook
Can Cook!

Snook is a crook.

Snook the crook
lives by the brook.

Snook the crook
reads a book
by the brook.

While Snook the crook
reads his book
by the brook,
a fish grabs his hook.

Snook the crook,
who lives by the brook,
puts down his book
so that he can cook
the fish from the hook!

About SandCastle™

A professional team of educators, reading specialists, and content developers created the SandCastle™ series to support young readers as they develop reading skills and strategies and increase their general knowledge. The SandCastle™ series has four levels that correspond to early literacy development in young children. The levels are provided to help teachers and parents select the appropriate books for young readers.

Emerging Readers
(no flags)

Beginning Readers
(1 flag)

Transitional Readers
(2 flags)

Fluent Readers
(3 flags)

These levels are meant only as a guide. All levels are subject to change.

To see a complete list of SandCastle™ books and other nonfiction titles from ABDO Publishing Company, visit **www.abdopub.com** or contact us at: 4940 Viking Drive, Edina, Minnesota 55435 • 1-800-800-1312 • fax: 1-952-831-1632